INSIDE THE NFL

KANSAS CITY CHIEFS

by Charlie Beattie

Abdo & Daughters
MIDDLE GRADE NONFICTION

An imprint of Abdo Publishing
abdobooks.com

ABDOBOOKS.COM

Published by Abdo Publishing, a division of ABDO, PO Box 398166, Minneapolis, Minnesota 55439.

Printed in China.
052025
092025

THIS BOOK CONTAINS RECYCLED MATERIALS

Cover Photos: Ezra Shaw/Getty Images Sport/Getty Images (Patrick Mahomes); Focus on Sport/Getty Images Sport/Getty Images (Derrick Thomas)
Interior Photos: Ryan Kang/Getty Images Sport/Getty Images, 4–5; David Durochik/AP Images, 6; Stacy Revere/Getty Images Sport/Getty Images, 7; David Eulitt/Getty Images Sport/Getty Images, 8, 50; Michael Reaves/Getty Images Sport/Getty Images, 9; Abdo Publishing, 10–11, 56; Bettmann/Getty Images, 12–13, 15, 22; Focus on Sport/Getty Images, 14; AP Images, 17, 60 (bottom left); Rich von Biberstein/Icon Sportswire/Getty Images, 18; Tony Tomsic/AP Images, 19, 28, 60 (top); Michael Ochs Archives/Moviepix/Getty Images, 20; James Flores/Getty Images Sport/Getty Images, 21; Focus on Sport/Getty Images Sport/Getty Images, 23, 26, 31, 32, 36–37, 60 (bottom right); Vernon Biever/AP Images, 24–25; James Drake/Getty Images Sport/Getty Images, 27; George Gojkovich/Getty Images Sport/Getty Images, 29, 30; Chuck Solomon/AP Images, 33; Mitchell Layton/Getty Images Sport/Getty Images, 34; Kirby Lee/Getty Images Sport/Getty Images, 35, 45; David Stluka/AP Images, 38, 39, 61 (top left); Paul Spinelli/NFL Photos/AP Images, 40; G. Newman Lowrance/AP Images, 41, 46; Paul Spinelli/AP Images, 42, 61 (bottom left); Elsa/Getty Images Sport/Getty Images, 43; Rick Osentoski/AP Images, 44; Joel Auerbach/Getty Images Sport/Getty Images, 48–49; Kevin Terrell/AP Images, 51, 63; Matthew Stockman/Getty Images Sport/Getty Images, 52; Michael Zagaris/San Francisco 49ers/Getty Images Sport/Getty Images, 53; Carmen Mandato/Getty Images Sport/Getty Images, 55, 61 (top right); Gregory Shamus/Getty Images Sport/Getty Images, 57; Patrick Smith/Getty Images Sport/Getty Images, 58; Perry Knotts/Getty Images Sport/Getty Images, 59, 61 (bottom right)

Editor: Rebecca Higgins
Series Designer: Laura Graphenteen
Production Designer: Laura Kuchar

Library of Congress Control Number: 2024948504

Publisher's Cataloging-in-Publication Data

Names: Beattie, Charlie, author.
Title: Kansas City Chiefs / by Charlie Beattie
Description: Minneapolis, Minnesota: Abdo Publishing, 2026 | Series: Inside the NFL | Includes online resources and index.
Identifiers: ISBN 9781098296773 (lib. bdg.) | ISBN 9798384919292 (ebook)
Subjects: LCSH: Kansas City Chiefs (Football team)--Juvenile literature. | National Football League--Juvenile literature. | Football teams--Juvenile literature. | American football--Juvenile literature.
Classification: DDC 796.33264--dc23

CONTENTS

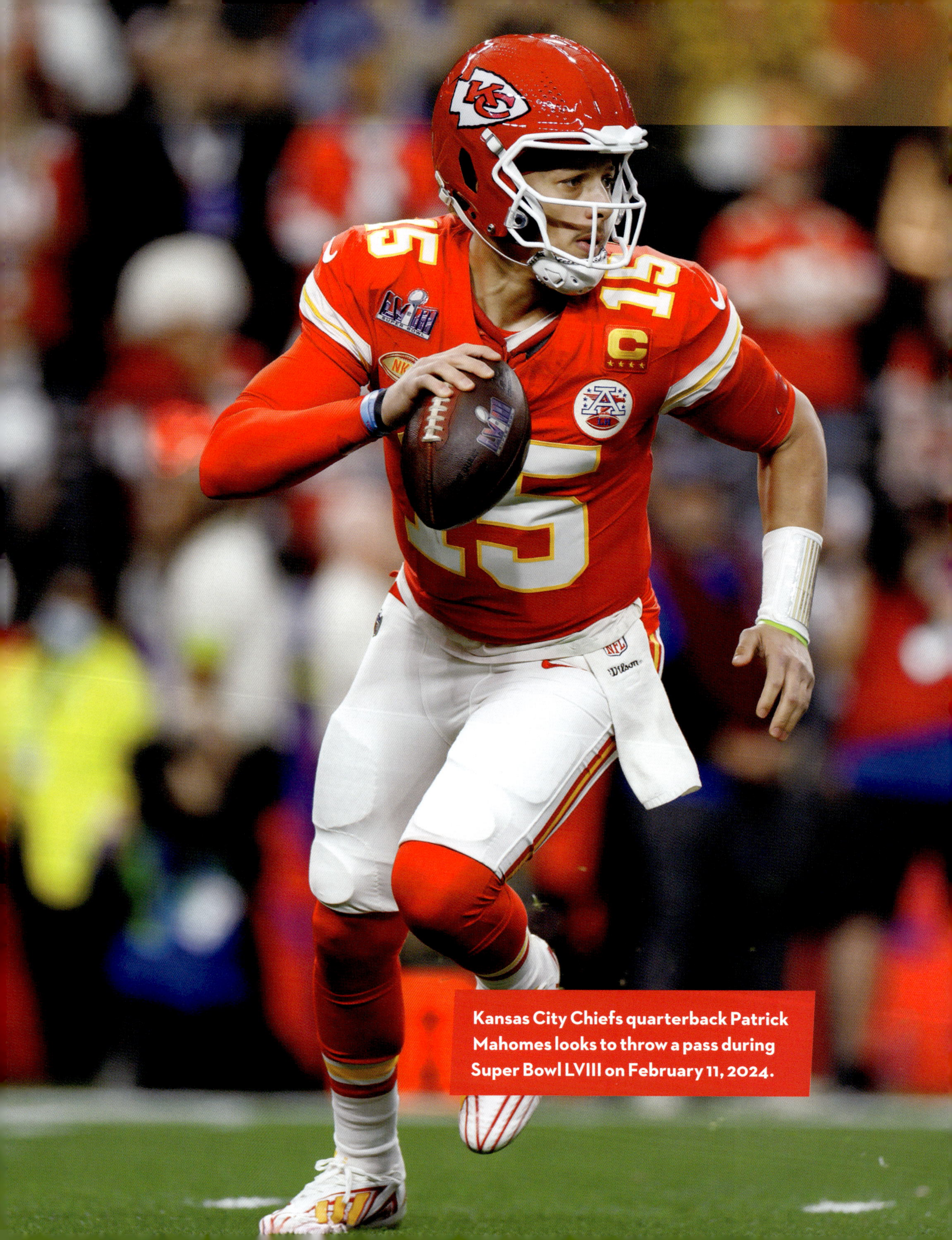

Kansas City Chiefs quarterback Patrick Mahomes looks to throw a pass during Super Bowl LVIII on February 11, 2024.

CHAPTER 1

CEMENTING A DYNASTY

THE PRESSURE WAS ON PATRICK MAHOMES AS THE CLOCK WOUND DOWN in overtime of Super Bowl LVIII. Mahomes and the Kansas City Chiefs were down 22-19 to the San Francisco 49ers on February 11, 2024. The quarterback stood in the shotgun formation. Kansas City was 3 yards from becoming one of the greatest dynasties in National Football League (NFL) history.

Mahomes looked to his right. He then waved his right arm, signaling wide receiver Mecole Hardman to go into motion. Hardman, on the right side of the formation, jogged toward the end of the offensive line. As soon as he got there, Mahomes took the snap. The Chiefs had timed the pre-snap segment of the play to perfection. They just had to finish it off and make history.

JOINING THE GREATS

The NFL has a long history of Super Bowl dynasties. The Green Bay Packers began the tradition by winning the first two Super Bowls after the 1966 and 1967 seasons. In the 1970s, the Pittsburgh Steelers won three Super Bowls. Since then, an NFL team has won at least three Super Bowls in each decade. The San Francisco 49ers followed in the 1980s, then the Dallas Cowboys did it in the 1990s. Next up, the New England Patriots strung together two dynasties, winning six Super Bowls between the 2001 and 2018 seasons. By then, however, a new dynasty was forming in Kansas City.

The Chiefs nearly toppled the Patriots in the American Football Conference (AFC) title game after the 2018 season. Kansas City scored 24 points in the fourth quarter but lost 37–31 in overtime. While the Patriots went on to claim their sixth title, Kansas City proved to be a tough competitor.

Chiefs head coach Andy Reid was considered one of the best offensive minds ever in the NFL. Reid had a dynamic quarterback, Mahomes. The young star's highlight-reel throws stunned fans. Travis Kelce, a big and athletic tight end, was often ready to receive Mahomes's passes. Together, that trio led Kansas City to its first Super Bowl in 50 years after the 2019 season. It was just the start of the Chiefs' dynasty.

Super Bowl LVIII marked the fourth championship game in five years for the Chiefs. They had added a second title in Super Bowl LVII after the 2022 season. Then, with a win over the talented 49ers, the Chiefs could cement their status as one of the NFL's all-time great Super Bowl teams.

Tight end Travis Kelce, *left*, celebrates a touchdown with Mahomes in 2019.

A THRILLING FINISH

As Mahomes took the shotgun snap, Hardman stopped his progress and broke back toward the sideline. Hardman's defender followed his every move. Meanwhile, Kelce jogged forward as if he were running a pass pattern. When the 49ers' cornerback tried to chase Hardman, the defender ran straight into Kelce. Reid's play call had worked exactly as he hoped. Hardman was wide-open.

Mahomes rolled out to his right and fired a pass directly between the numbers of Hardman's No. 12 jersey. The receiver caught the pass for a championship-clinching touchdown. He then lifted the ball high above his head. Mahomes raced into the end zone, where Hardman jumped into his quarterback's arms. Soon the rest of the team rushed to join in celebration.

The thrilling win was the Chiefs' third Super Bowl title in five years. Mahomes was only 28 years old. Reid was still

HARDMAN THE HERO

The Chiefs selected Mecole Hardman in the second round of the 2019 NFL Draft. After three productive seasons, Hardman was injured and kept out of the 2022 lineup. Before the 2023 season, Hardman became a free agent. After playing five games for the New York Jets, Hardman was traded back to the Chiefs in the middle of the season. Between the regular season and playoffs, he caught only 19 passes for the Chiefs, and his only touchdown was the Super Bowl winner.

The Chiefs celebrate Mecole Hardman's game-winning touchdown reception in Super Bowl LVIII.

pulling the offensive strings from the sideline. And with talented players at just about every position, the Chiefs' dynasty looked as if it was just getting started.

NFL TEAMS MAP

NFC

NFC EAST

- DALLAS COWBOYS
- NEW YORK GIANTS
- PHILADELPHIA EAGLES
- WASHINGTON COMMANDERS

NFC WEST

- ARIZONA CARDINALS
- LOS ANGELES RAMS
- SAN FRANCISCO 49ERS
- SEATTLE SEAHAWKS

NFC NORTH

- CHICAGO BEARS
- DETROIT LIONS
- GREEN BAY PACKERS
- MINNESOTA VIKINGS

NFC SOUTH

- ATLANTA FALCONS
- CAROLINA PANTHERS
- NEW ORLEANS SAINTS
- TAMPA BAY BUCCANEERS

AFC

AFC EAST

- BUFFALO BILLS
- MIAMI DOLPHINS
- NEW ENGLAND PATRIOTS
- NEW YORK JETS

AFC WEST

- DENVER BRONCOS
- KANSAS CITY CHIEFS
- LAS VEGAS RAIDERS
- LOS ANGELES CHARGERS

AFC NORTH

- BALTIMORE RAVENS
- CINCINNATI BENGALS
- CLEVELAND BROWNS
- PITTSBURGH STEELERS

AFC SOUTH

- HOUSTON TEXANS
- INDIANAPOLIS COLTS
- JACKSONVILLE JAGUARS
- TENNESSEE TITANS

Lamar Hunt, *right*, created the team that became the Kansas City Chiefs.

CHAPTER 2

DALLAS DEBUT

THE KANSAS CITY CHIEFS ARE ONE OF THE NFL'S MOST STORIED franchises. However, the team began far away from Kansas City. It also started in an entirely different league.

In 1959, Dallas businessman Lamar Hunt wanted nothing more than an NFL team in his city. However, a previous team there called the Dallas Texans had lasted just one season. The league's owners refused to let Hunt bring a team back to Dallas. Instead, Hunt decided to start a new league. Hunt and Houston businessman Bud Adams rounded up six other owners. The group, who called themselves the Foolish Club, founded the American Football League (AFL). Hunt decided to call his new team the Texans.

The 27-year-old Hunt hired Hank Stram to coach his team. During training camp before the inaugural 1960 season, Stram delivered his first speech to the Texans. Stram admitted he didn't know how long the AFL would last, but that he wanted the Texans to lead the league.

THE LONGEST GAME

The Texans fell short of Stram's goal at first, finishing a combined 14–14 over their first two seasons. But Dallas fielded the AFL's best running back in Abner Haynes. In 1962, the team signed quarterback Len Dawson to connect with the speedy Haynes. Dawson had been a top NFL draft pick in 1957. But in his five years with the Pittsburgh Steelers and Cleveland Browns, he had started only two games. Hunt had little faith that the quarterback would do more in Dallas. Instead, Dawson was an instant hit. He led the AFL with

Quarterback Len Dawson (16) led the AFL in completion percentage seven times between 1962 and 1969.

29 touchdown passes in 1962 and led Dallas to an 11–3 finish. The Texans faced off against the two-time defending league champion Houston Oilers in the title game.

Despite playing at Houston and in windy conditions, Haynes and Dawson were determined. The pair hooked up for a 28-yard touchdown pass early in the second quarter. Haynes then scored on a 2-yard rush as Dallas built a 17–0 halftime lead. However, the Oilers rallied in the second half, tying the game 17–17 and forcing overtime.

The team captains met on the field for the coin toss. The winner could either choose to receive, kick off, or defend a certain end of the field. But they couldn't choose more than one option. Stiff winds were blowing toward one end of Houston's Jeppesen Stadium, which featured a scoreboard and the game clock. Stram wanted to defend the opposite goal, so Dallas would have to drive into the wind.

But after Dallas won the toss, Haynes mistakenly said, "We'll kick to the clock." Stram lost his strategic move. Houston got the ball but would have to battle the wind.

Running back Abner Haynes scored both Dallas touchdowns in the 1962 AFL Championship Game.

The Texans' defense took the field. Dallas's defense, led by All-Pros such as linebacker E. J. Holub and defensive back Bobby Hunt, stood firm at first. The Texans forced a second overtime period.

"I'VE NEVER SEEN A TEAM WORK HARDER TO WIN A FOOTBALL GAME."

—HANK STRAM

With the wind now at their backs, the Texans drove inside the Houston 20. Dallas kicker Tommy Brooker hit a field goal with 12:06 left in the second extra session to win the title. At the time, it was the longest game in football history. Stram praised his team for overcoming Haynes's coin toss mistake. He said, "I've never seen a team work harder to win a football game."

ON THE MOVE

The Texans were champions, but their future in Dallas was uncertain. When Lamar Hunt announced his AFL would have a team in Dallas, the NFL had responded by forming the Dallas Cowboys in 1960. To make matters worse, the Dallas teams shared the cavernous 76,000-seat Cotton Bowl. Only one team could play in it each Sunday, so the other had to hit the road. But many Dallas fans opted not to attend home games and watched the Cowboys' road games on TV. By 1962, Hunt was often giving away tickets to Texans games. The team was losing so much money that he decided to move out of his hometown.

Hunt considered moving his team to Seattle, Atlanta, New Orleans, or Miami. Instead, the mayor of Kansas City, Missouri, won him over. The mayor, H. Roe Bartle, was nicknamed "Chief," though he was not American Indian. Before the 1963 season, Hunt rehomed

Teammates carry kicker Tommy Brooker off the field after his game-winning field goal in the 1962 AFL Championship Game.

The Chiefs' arrowhead logo has been on the team's helmets since 1963, but the team's use of American Indian imagery has caused controversy through the years.

his team in Missouri. The team was renamed the Kansas City Chiefs, in honor of Bartle.

Throughout the team's history, the name has led to issues. Many American Indian nations have found the team's name, mascot, and arrowhead logo offensive. They say it is disrespectful to their cultures. Indigenous peoples have also objected to fans wearing Native religious regalia such as headdresses. In recent years, Kansas City's owners have talked with some Native groups about better representing them. However, many Native and non-Native peoples have called on the team to change its name entirely.

SUPER BOWL BOUND

After missing the postseason for three straight years, the Chiefs returned in 1966. Dawson led the AFL in touchdown passes for the fourth time in five years. Most of his 26 scoring tosses went to either lanky second-year wide receiver Otis Taylor or deep threat Chris Burford. On the ground, rookie Mike Garrett rushed for more than 800 yards.

Wide receiver Otis Taylor caught 57 touchdown passes in 11 seasons with the Chiefs.

Cornerback Fred Williamson played for the Chiefs from 1965 to 1967.

The Chiefs' league-leading offense was complemented by an exceptional defense. Linebacker Bobby Bell joined Holub. They played behind Hall of Fame defensive tackle Buck Buchanan. The secondary featured star safeties Bobby Hunt and Johnny Robinson, who each intercepted 10 passes. Cornerback Fred Williamson was known as "the Hammer" for his thumping hits.

Kansas City defensive tackle Buck Buchanan (86) looks to make a tackle during Super Bowl I on January 15, 1967.

Kansas City finished 11–2–1. In the 1966 league championship, the Chiefs topped the Buffalo Bills 31–7. Up until that year, that would have been the end of the season. However, thanks in large part to Lamar Hunt, the AFL and the NFL had agreed to merge. They would officially become one league beginning with the 1970 season. But starting with the 1966 season, both leagues' champions would face off to determine an overall champion.

The Chiefs met the Green Bay Packers on January 15, 1967, in the AFL-NFL Championship Game. Hunt had seen his children playing with a toy called a Super Ball and had a name for the new championship game: the Super Bowl. The game between the Chiefs and the Packers is now known as Super Bowl I.

Kansas City was playing for a title. But the Chiefs also wanted respect. Since the AFL had been formed, critics had dismissed it as an inferior league. If the Chiefs could beat the Packers, they would prove the doubters wrong. However, few expected them to truly contend against a Green Bay team that had dominated the NFL throughout the 1960s.

The Packers scored the game's first touchdown. But the Chiefs immediately responded. Dawson threw a 7-yard scoring pass to fullback Curtis McClinton early in the second quarter. Green Bay then scored again. Late in the first half, Kansas City kicker Mike Mercer booted the Super Bowl's first-ever field goal. The Chiefs went into halftime down 14–10.

On Kansas City's first drive of the second half, Dawson threw an interception that was returned to the Chiefs' 5. The Packers scored on the next play to take a 21–10 lead. With the Chiefs struggling to move the ball, Green Bay added two more touchdowns to win 35–10. It was a bitter defeat and made worse by Packers' coach Vince Lombardi saying that the Chiefs didn't measure up to any NFL team. The Chiefs had been defeated, but they were hungry.

MACK LEE HILL

In 1964, Chiefs rookie Mack Lee Hill rushed for more than 500 yards. "The Truck" topped that in 13 games in 1965 before a knee injury ended his season. As Hill was undergoing knee surgery, he suffered a sudden embolism and died. To honor the back, Kansas City created the Mack Lee Hill Award. It is still given to the team's best rookie each year.

Mack Lee Hill averaged 5.2 yards per rush in his brief professional career.

Dawson threw for 211 yards and a touchdown during Super Bowl I.

Kansas City quarterback Mike Livingston threw for 1,123 yards in 1969.

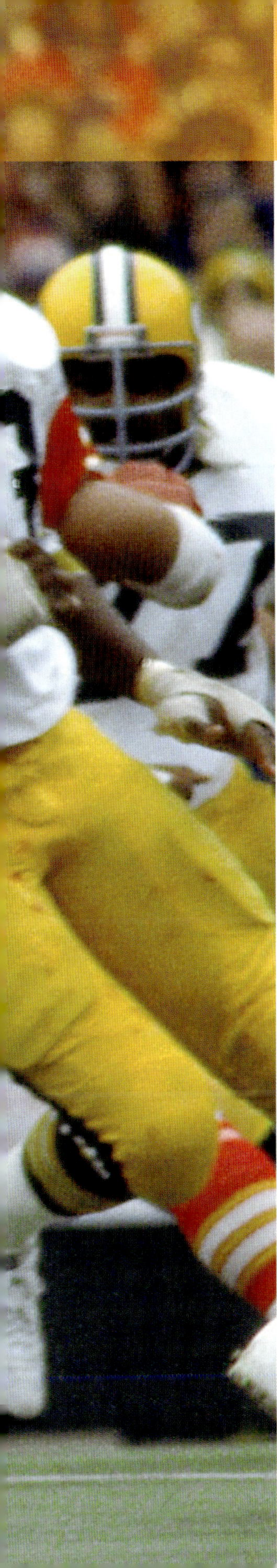

CHAPTER 3

CHAMPION CHIEFS

THE CHIEFS FOLLOWED UP THEIR SUPER BOWL APPEARANCE WITH two more winning seasons. But each fell short of another Super Bowl. Kansas City's chances of a successful 1969 season took a hit in its second game when quarterback Len Dawson went down with an injury. A week later, backup Jacky Lee was also hurt. In their absence, third-string quarterback Mike Livingston stepped up, securing five victories in a row. Dawson returned by Week 8 and started the season's five final games. With an 11–3 record, Kansas City headed back to the playoffs.

The Chiefs faced the defending Super Bowl champion New York Jets. The game was tied 6–6 when Dawson threw a late touchdown pass to receiver Gloster Richardson to win 13–6. The next week, Kansas City beat the division-rival

Oakland Raiders 17–7 in the AFL title game. For the second time in four years, the Chiefs were headed to the Super Bowl.

65 TOSS POWER TRAP

The Super Bowl had become a huge event. Before Super Bowl IV between the Chiefs and the Minnesota Vikings, NFL Films, the company that produces the league's videos, approached Minnesota coach Bud Grant. They asked him to wear a microphone during the game. Grant turned the idea down.

The producers also asked Hank Stram. He had worn a microphone during a regular-season game and agreed to do it again. As his underdog Chiefs took the field, every word Stram said was recorded.

Stram's sideline speeches were entertaining. During a first-half drive, he said, "Just keep matriculating the ball down the field, boys." Stram originated the term *matriculate* in football, which means "to advance." So Stram wanted his players to just focus on driving toward the end zone. Later, he approached an official and said calmly, "Mr. Official,

Hank Stram coached the Texans/Chiefs from 1960 to 1974.

let me ask you something." When the official told him to go ahead, Stram launched into a tirade, yelling "How could all six of you miss a play like that!"

Running back Mike Garrett celebrates in the end zone after scoring on the Chiefs' famous "65 Toss Power Trap" play in Super Bowl IV on January 11, 1970.

In the second quarter, the Chiefs ran a play that would become famous. Already up 9–0 after three field goals from Jan Stenerud, Kansas City had the ball at Minnesota's 5-yard line. Stram called for a play that the Chiefs hadn't even practiced in weeks, called "65 Toss Power Trap." On the play, Dawson faked a pitch to a running back heading to the outside. He then handed off to Mike Garrett. The star back had a huge hole up the middle and waltzed in for a touchdown. Stram, who had predicted the play would work, was cackling as his team came to the sideline.

Kansas City linebacker Willie Lanier (63) racked up four tackles and an interception during Super Bowl IV.

The team's defense, led by star linebacker Willie Lanier, caused five turnovers and sacked Vikings' quarterback Joe Kapp three times. Dawson and receiver Otis Taylor delivered the highlight play of the game on a 46-yard touchdown pass in the third quarter. The Chiefs laughed all the way to a 23–7 upset victory.

It was the AFL's second straight Super Bowl win. Kansas City accomplished the feat by dominating a strong NFL team. As the two leagues prepared to officially merge in 1970, there was no doubt that the AFL teams would be competitive with teams in the older league.

THE SLOW DECLINE

The Chiefs' first Super Bowl win was a thrilling time for the team. But Dawson was 34 years old when Kansas City beat the Vikings.

Halfback Ed Podolak put up 4,451 rushing yards and 2,456 receiving yards with the Chiefs from 1969 to 1977.

Over the next few seasons, his performance on the field continued to decline. Dawson threw only 15 touchdown passes in 1971, though he still led the team to a 10–3–1 record and a spot in the playoffs.

In the divisional round against the Miami Dolphins, versatile halfback Ed Podolak piled up more than 300 all-purpose yards and scored two touchdowns. With the teams tied 24–24 late in the game, Podolak drove the Chiefs down the field. Stenerud then missed a chance to win the game on a would-be last-second field goal. After both teams missed field goals in the first overtime, the game went to a second extra period. It passed the 1962 AFL Championship Game as the longest game ever. With 7:20 left in the second overtime, Miami kicked a field goal and won 27–24.

Defensive end Art Still (67) joined the Chiefs in 1978 and totaled 74 sacks in 10 years with the team.

The Chiefs had winning records the next two seasons but didn't reach the playoffs. Stram stepped down after a 5–9 season in 1974. The talkative coach led the New Orleans Saints for two years before a long career as a radio and TV announcer. After the 1975 season, Dawson retired. Without its two leaders, Kansas City continued to decline, finally bottoming out by finishing 2–12 in 1977.

The next season, Kansas City hired Marv Levy as its new head coach. Levy knew his team struggled to pass the ball. Instead, he decided to focus on the ground game. By 1981, the Chiefs were one of the top rushing teams in the NFL. Rookie running back Joe Delaney was a major driver behind that. Despite a small 5-foot-10-inch, 184-pound frame, Delaney wowed fans by rushing for 1,121 yards and three touchdowns in just 15 games. Opponents compared him to all-time great backs such as Walter Payton and Gale Sayers. However, even Delaney's heroics weren't enough to end Kansas City's playoff drought. The team finished 9–7, but that was only good enough for third place in the AFC West.

Chiefs' fans never found out just how good Delaney might have been. Before the 1983 season, Delaney was home in Monroe, Louisiana, when he heard three drowning children calling for help. Delaney couldn't swim but jumped into the water anyway. While managing to save one of the children, Delaney drowned.

No Chiefs player has worn No. 37 since running back Joe Delaney's death in 1983.

RETURN TO THE PLAYOFFS

The Chiefs had struggled to find a quarterback after Dawson retired. The 1983 draft featured several talented rookies. Six quarterbacks ended up

Quarterback Bill Kenney threw 24 touchdowns in 1983.

being taken in the first round. Kansas City selected one of them, Todd Blackledge, with the seventh pick.

Blackledge struggled through the next few seasons. He frequently split time with veteran Bill Kenney. In 1983, Kenney led

Nose tackle Bill Maas was the Chiefs' top draft pick in 1984.

the league with 346 completed passes and earned a spot in the Pro Bowl.

The Chiefs built a strong defense under new coach John Mackovic, who arrived in 1983. By 1986, that all came together. Nose tackle Bill Maas was stuffing opposing running backs. In the secondary, cornerbacks Kevin Ross and Albert Lewis each grabbed

Safety Deron Cherry was named to the All-Pro team three times while playing for the Chiefs.

four interceptions. Safeties Lloyd Burruss and Deron Cherry had a combined total of 14. Both Burruss and Cherry made the Pro Bowl.

On the final day of the regular season, Kansas City traveled to face the Pittsburgh Steelers. A win would clinch the Chiefs' first playoff spot in 15 years. Pittsburgh had 515 yards to the Chiefs' 171. But Kansas City's defense and special teams came to the rescue. In the first quarter, Cherry dived on a blocked punt in the end zone for a 7–0 lead. With Kansas City up 10–3 in the second quarter, Chiefs' kick returner Boyce Green took a kickoff back 97 yards for a score. With the score 17–6 in the third, Burruss scooped up a blocked kick and raced 78 yards for a touchdown. Despite not scoring an offensive touchdown in the game, the Chiefs won 24–19.

The team's playoff stay didn't last long. In the wild-card round, Blackledge filled in for injured Kenney and threw a pair of interceptions. The Jets rocked Kansas City 35–15. The playoff drought was over, but the Chiefs had a lot of work to do to contend for titles again.

ARROWHEAD STADIUM

After a decade playing in Municipal Stadium, the Chiefs opened Arrowhead Stadium in 1974. The open-air stadium quickly became known as one of the loudest in the NFL. In one 1990 game, fans were so loud that the referee threatened to charge the Chiefs with a timeout if fans didn't quiet down. In 2014, Kansas City fans set a record of 142 decibels, which is as loud as fireworks, with their cheering against the New England Patriots.

Chiefs running back Christian Okoye rushed for career highs of 1,480 yards and 12 touchdowns in 1989.

CHAPTER 4

WINNING WAYS

THE CHIEFS HAD ONE HEAD COACH, HANK STRAM, FOR THEIR FIRST 15 seasons. From 1975 to 1988, they went through five. In 1989, Marty Schottenheimer became the sixth new sideline boss in Kansas City.

Schottenheimer favored a strong defense and an offense focused on running. In Kansas City, he had both. On offense, Nigerian-born running back Christian Okoye was a load to tackle. At 6 feet, 1 inch and 253 pounds, the back pummeled his way to the rushing title in 1989.

That same year, Chiefs' first-round draft pick Derrick Thomas recorded 10 sacks. It was the start of a Hall of Fame career for the speedy linebacker. Over the next decade, he was one of the most entertaining defensive players

“WHEN DERRICK IS AT THE TOP OF HIS GAME, HE’S ONE OF THE MOST DOMINATING FORCES IN FOOTBALL.”

—DAN WILLIAMS

in football. In 11 seasons, Thomas racked up a team-record 126 1/2 sacks.

He also had a knack for knocking the ball loose. Thomas forced 45 fumbles in his career. Teammate Dan Williams noted that, “Without question, when Derrick is at the top of his game, he’s one of the most dominating forces in football.”

DERRICK THOMAS’S BIG DAY

On November 11, 1990, Derrick Thomas pummeled Seattle Seahawks quarterback Dave Krieg. With seven sacks, Thomas set the NFL single-game sack record. However, on the game’s final play, Krieg shook free from what would have been Thomas’s eighth sack and threw a touchdown pass to win the game 17–16. Thomas was proud of the record, but later said the deciding play was the one thing from his career he wished he could change.

Derrick Thomas was named to the Pro Bowl nine times in his career.

Thomas’s best season was 1990. The second-year man recorded 20 sacks as Kansas City went back to the playoffs. In the wild-card round, Okoye rushed for 83 yards. But the Chiefs threw away a 16–3 fourth-quarter lead and lost 17–16 to the Miami Dolphins.

Under Schottenheimer, the Chiefs became a regular playoff team. But winning in the postseason was tougher. Kansas City still didn’t have a star quarterback. After losing in 1991 with Steve DeBerg under center and a year later with veteran Dave Krieg, Kansas City made a few bold moves before the 1993 season.

ADDING LEGENDS

Joe Montana was already an NFL legend by 1993. The 37-year-old quarterback had led the San Francisco 49ers to four Super Bowls between the 1981 and 1989 seasons. However, in 1993, he was coming off two seasons in which he had played only one game due to an arm injury. The Chiefs took a chance and traded for him anyway.

Quarterback Joe Montana threw 29 touchdowns in two seasons with the Chiefs.

Kansas City also brought in star running back Marcus Allen, who had been playing for the rival Los Angeles Raiders. To block for both new weapons, general manager Carl Peterson drafted punishing rookie guard Will Shields. With three future Hall of Famers then on offense, the Chiefs finished 11–5. Montana threw 13 touchdown passes in 11 games. Allen added 12 rushing scores. The Chiefs won the AFC West for the first time since 1971.

In the wild-card round, Montana and Allen led a fourth-quarter comeback against the Pittsburgh Steelers. Kansas City tied the game with a late touchdown pass. Chiefs' kicker Nick Lowery scored an overtime field goal to win it 27–24.

Running back Marcus Allen ran for 44 touchdowns with the Chiefs from 1993 to 1997.

In a tough divisional-round matchup against the physical Houston Oilers, Allen rushed for 74 yards and his late touchdown sealed a 28–20 Kansas City win. That sent the Chiefs to their first American Football Conference (AFC) title game. However, the run ended there with a 30–13 loss to the Buffalo Bills.

SUPERSTARS AND X-FACTORS

Montana retired after the 1994 season, but Kansas City remained successful—at least in the regular season. In 1995, the Chiefs won

13 games. They did it again two years later. But in both years, Kansas City fell short of the Super Bowl.

When Schottenheimer left the team after the 1998 season, the Chiefs promoted defensive coordinator Gunther Cunningham. But after two years, Kansas City replaced him with veteran head coach Dick Vermeil in 2001. He took over an offense that featured one of the NFL's best tight ends. The Chiefs had drafted

Tony Gonzalez retired as the NFL's all-time leading pass catcher among tight ends.

Tony Gonzalez with the 13th pick in 1997. At 6 feet, 5 inches and 247 pounds, he was a great athlete. In college, Gonzalez starred in both football and basketball. With his quick moves and soft hands, he rewrote Kansas City's receiving record book over his 12 seasons. By the time he left the Chiefs, Gonzalez had caught 916 passes for more than 10,000 yards and 76 touchdowns.

In addition to his record-setting rushing totals, running back Priest Holmes caught 206 passes for 1,976 yards between 2001 and 2003.

Gonzalez was far from the Chiefs' only offensive weapon. Running back Priest Holmes had been a backup with the Baltimore Ravens in the late 1990s. He joined the Chiefs in 2001 and immediately led the NFL in rushing with a team-record 1,555 yards. In 2002, he broke that record and topped the league with 24 total touchdowns. A year later, he had an NFL-record 27 rushing scores.

Dante Hall was an undersized receiver. In 2000, he served as a kick returner for five games. Next year, when Vermeil took over as head coach, Hall had earned the kick returner job. Between 2002 and 2004, Hall's electrifying returns lit up the NFL. The 5-foot, 8-inch Hall had two nicknames. The first was "the Human Joystick," as his slippery moves reminded fans of a video game. The second was "the X-Factor." In 2003, Hall returned either a punt or a kickoff for a touchdown in four consecutive games.

The Chiefs rode their strong offense to a 9–0 start in 2003 before finishing 13–3. As AFC West champions, the Chiefs hosted the Indianapolis Colts in the divisional round. Though the Colts bottled up Gonzalez, holding the star tight end to just four catches,

Receiver Dante Hall races past a defender on his 92-yard kickoff return against the Indianapolis Colts in the playoffs after the 2003 season.

Holmes scored twice, and Hall caught a touchdown pass. Peyton Manning's touchdown pass late in the third quarter put Indianapolis up 31–17. On the following kickoff, Hall caught the ball at the Chiefs' 8-yard line. After starting left, Hall cut back through the middle of the field, weaving through traffic for a 92-yard touchdown. Arrowhead Stadium erupted. But Hall's return was not enough. The Chiefs lost 38–31.

BAD RECORDS

When a back injury slowed Holmes down in 2005, Larry Johnson took over as the Chiefs' top runner. Johnson quickly smashed Holmes's team record by rushing for 1,750 yards. The next year, Johnson piled up 1,789 more. That total helped Kansas City return

Running back Jamaal Charles (25) led the NFL with 12 touchdown runs in 2013.

Guard Will Shields (68) started 223 of 224 career games with the Chiefs before retiring in 2006.

Kansas City quarterback Alex Smith throws a pass during the team's defeat against the Colts on January 4, 2014.

to the playoffs for the first time in three years. But once again facing the Colts, the Chiefs struggled. Indianapolis bottled up Johnson, holding him to 32 yards on 13 carries as Kansas City fell 23–8.

Johnson never again performed as well as he had in 2005 and 2006. Soon he was replaced by Jamaal Charles. As a high school track star, he ran the 100 meters in 10.1 seconds and claimed four All-American titles in college. Charles sped past NFL defenders. He topped 1,000 rushing yards five times between 2009 and 2014 to become Kansas City's all-time leading rusher. However, the team struggled to find consistent quarterbacks. Charles played in only two playoff games as a Chief.

The second of those games was one of the team's lowest points. In 2013, the Chiefs hired Andy Reid as head coach. Known as one of the best offensive minds in the NFL, Reid had taken the Philadelphia Eagles to the Super Bowl after the 2004 season. But since then, he had a history of coming up short in the playoffs.

After Kansas City finished 11–5, the team traveled to face the Colts in yet another postseason matchup. Chiefs quarterback Alex Smith threw four touchdowns to build a 38–10 lead early in the third quarter. Then the Chiefs' defense, which had been strong all season, just needed to hold on. But the team suffered a handful of injuries in that game. Score by score, the Colts clawed their way back to win 45–44. It was the second-largest collapse in playoff history. The loss was also Kansas City's eighth postseason loss in a row, an NFL record. But better days were right around the corner.

The Chiefs took tight end Travis Kelce with the 63rd pick in the 2013 draft.

CHAPTER 5

KANSAS CITY DYNASTY

ANDY REID RECOVERED FROM THE PLAYOFF DISASTER IN HIS FIRST season to slowly build an excellent team. Before the 2013 season, Kansas City had drafted a little-known tight end from the University of Cincinnati named Travis Kelce in the third round. Kelce barely played his rookie year due to a knee injury. But by the time the Chiefs reached the playoffs again in 2015, he was one of quarterback Alex Smith's top targets. In the wild-card round, Kelce led the Chiefs with eight catches for 128 yards. Kansas City rocked the Houston Texans 30–0, finally ending their playoff losing streak.

The Chiefs lost in the divisional round to the powerhouse New England Patriots, but more talent was on the way. In the 2016 draft, the team used its top pick on defensive tackle Chris Jones, who went on to become one of the league's most

Defensive tackle Chris Jones was named to the All-Pro team for the first time in 2022.

dominant defensive players. In the fifth round, the Chiefs nabbed undersized receiver Tyreek Hill. Though only 5 feet, 10 inches, Hill used his speed to become one of Reid's top offensive weapons.

MVP MAHOMES

In 2016, the Chiefs won the AFC West. Smith, a former number one overall draft pick, was a solid quarterback. With so much talent around him, the Chiefs were a team on the rise. But after losing 18–16 to the Pittsburgh Steelers in the divisional playoffs, Kansas City made a bold decision in the 2017 NFL Draft. The Chiefs traded up 17 spots to take quarterback Patrick Mahomes 10th overall.

At the time, some scouts didn't believe Mahomes would perform well in the NFL. The son of a former professional baseball pitcher, and an excellent baseball player himself, Mahomes was clocked throwing a football at 60 miles per hour (97 km/h). He had played in a wide-open offensive system at Texas Tech. Many quarterbacks before him had also put up huge numbers as Red Raiders, but none had been successful at the professional level.

Through the first 100 games of his NFL career, Patrick Mahomes averaged 293.3 passing yards per game, the highest average in NFL history.

His rifle of a right arm was just one reason why Mahomes was soon the talk of the NFL. Reid knew Mahomes needed time to adjust. As a rookie, Mahomes sat on the bench and watched the veteran Smith. In 2018, Mahomes got the starting job.

In Mahomes's first year as a starter, he led the NFL with an incredible 50 touchdown passes. But it wasn't just his numbers. Mahomes threw passes that few other quarterbacks would dare try. He often tossed the ball to receivers he wasn't even looking at. On one play against the Denver Broncos, the right-handed quarterback was being pulled down by a defender. Using his left hand, Mahomes threw the ball 10 yards downfield to Hill.

The Chiefs excited fans as they finished 12–4. They reached the AFC title game, where they lost 37–31 in an overtime thriller to the Patriots. After the season, Mahomes became the first player in Chiefs history to win the league's Most Valuable Player (MVP) Award.

THE WAIT IS OVER

Mahomes's numbers dipped in 2019 as he missed a pair of games due to injury. But the Chiefs finished 12–4 to win the AFC West for the fourth straight year. In the divisional playoffs, they fell behind the visiting Texans 24–0 in the second quarter. However, the Chiefs' offense showed its explosiveness by scoring four touchdowns before halftime. Kansas City rolled to a 51–31 victory. In the AFC title game, Kansas City was down 17–7 to the Tennessee Titans in the first half. Again, the Chiefs rallied. They won 35–24.

With the win, the Chiefs reached the Super Bowl for

Head coach Andy Reid, *left*, holds up the Lamar Hunt Trophy, which is given to the AFC champion each year.

the first time in 50 years. But facing a talented San Francisco 49ers team, Kansas City once again fell behind. The Chiefs trailed 20–10 in the fourth quarter. They faced third-and-15 at their own 35.

Mahomes dialed up a play called "2-3 Jet Chip Wasp." Hill sprinted down the middle of the field. Mahomes was hit but still connected with his star receiver on a 44-yard pass. Four plays later, Mahomes hit Kelce on a 1-yard touchdown pass. The Chiefs quickly got the ball back and drove to the San Francisco 5. There, Mahomes tossed a scoring strike to running back Damien Williams to take the lead. Kansas City went on to win 31–20.

Receiver Tyreek Hill grabs a key 44-yard pass late in Super Bowl LIV against the San Francisco 49ers in February 2020.

"WE HAVE HEART. WE NEVER GIVE UP."

—PATRICK MAHOMES

The Chiefs were Super Bowl champions for the first time since the AFL-NFL merger. And the victory showed that the Chiefs were never out of any game. "We have heart," Mahomes said after the game. "We never give up and those guys around us, the leaders on the team, have that mindset that we never give up."

COMEBACK KINGS

After winning Super Bowl LIV, the Chiefs appeared to be a potential dynasty. However, their plans were disrupted the next year when the Tampa Bay Buccaneers rocked them 31–9 in Super Bowl LV. A year later, the Chiefs led the AFC title game 21–3 against the Cincinnati Bengals before falling apart and losing 27–24. Instead of running it back in 2022, the Chiefs traded Hill to the Miami Dolphins.

Mahomes didn't miss a beat without his star receiver. He led the NFL with 5,250 yards passing and 41 touchdowns on his way to a second MVP Award. But in the divisional playoffs, Mahomes was hit by a Jacksonville Jaguars defender during a throw and injured his knee. Instead of another playoff disappointment, though, he came back to lead the team to a 27–20 win. He then limped his way through the AFC title game. With time running out, Mahomes drove the Chiefs into Cincinnati territory, setting up kicker Harrison Butker's last-second field goal to beat the Bengals 23–20.

In Super Bowl LVII, the Chiefs fell behind once again. Mahomes reinjured his knee on a second-quarter hit, and Kansas City trailed the Philadelphia Eagles 24–14 at halftime. Fighting through the pain, Mahomes rallied Kansas City to a 35–27 lead with just over

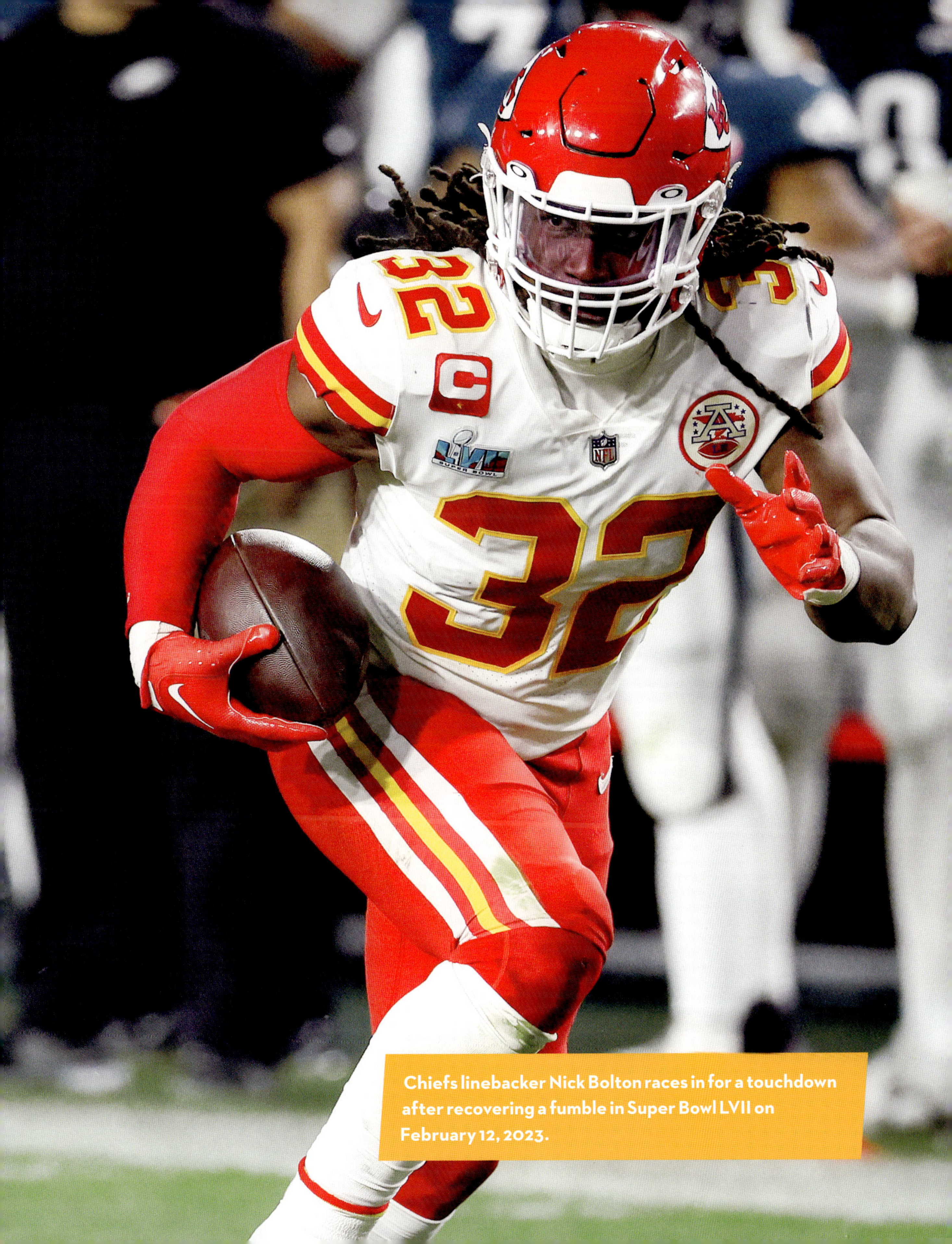

Chiefs linebacker Nick Bolton races in for a touchdown after recovering a fumble in Super Bowl LVII on February 12, 2023.

CHIEFS TROPHY CASE

SUPER BOWL CHAMPIONSHIPS: 4

Super Bowl IV – January 11, 1970
Super Bowl LIV – February 2, 2020
Super Bowl LVII – February 12, 2023
Super Bowl LVIII – February 11, 2024

AFL CHAMPIONSHIPS: 3

1962, 1966, 1969

CONFERENCE CHAMPIONSHIPS: 5

2019, 2020, 2022, 2023, 2024

DIVISION TITLES: 18

AFL West: 1962, 1966, 1968
AFC West: 1971, 1993, 1995, 1997, 2003, 2010, 2016, 2017, 2018, 2019, 2020, 2021, 2022, 2023, 2024

All stats are through the 2024 season.

nine minutes to play. The Eagles tied the game, but then Mahomes went to work on another drive. With just under three minutes left, the hurt quarterback scrambled for 26 yards. The play helped set up a 27-yard field-goal attempt with 11 seconds left. Butker's kick was good. The Chiefs won 38–35 and were champions again.

DYNASTY

The Chiefs entered 2023 looking to achieve something no NFL team had done in 20 years. They wanted to win back-to-back Super Bowls. Kansas City had the star power to make it happen. Mahomes had become the league's most recognizable player.

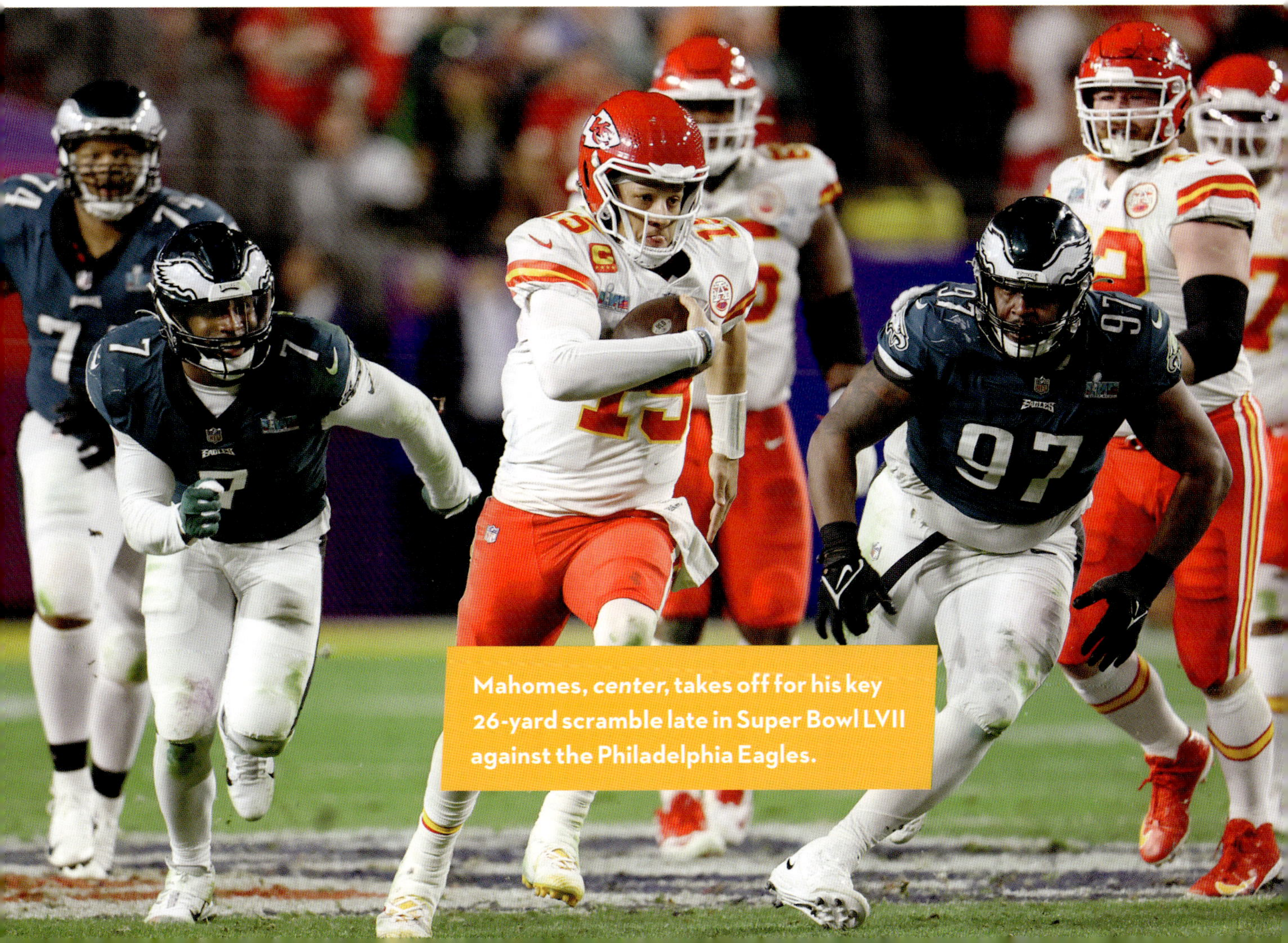

Mahomes, *center*, takes off for his key 26-yard scramble late in Super Bowl LVII against the Philadelphia Eagles.

Kelce was on the verge of breaking Tony Gonzalez's team receiving records.

Though the Chiefs won 11 games in 2023, they weren't as dominant as in previous seasons. But once again, they came through in the playoffs. After a comfortable win over the Dolphins, the Chiefs survived close calls against the Buffalo Bills and Baltimore Ravens to once again reach the Super Bowl.

Like Kansas City, the 49ers were loaded on offense. The 49ers built a 10–0 lead in the first half, but the Chiefs rallied again to take a 13–10 lead late in the third quarter. The offenses battled in the final quarter, and San Francisco took a 19–16 lead with 1:53 left. As he had done so many times before, Mahomes coolly led the Chiefs down the field. With 16 seconds left at the San Francisco 33, he tossed a short pass to Kelce, who raced down the sideline for 22 yards. Butker tied the game as

TAYLOR AND TRAVIS

Taylor Swift became the NFL's most famous fan after she started dating Travis Kelce before the 2023 season. The music superstar was a regular at Chiefs' games. She even raced back from one of her Eras Tour concerts in Japan to watch Super Bowl LVIII in February 2024. Swift's presence had a positive impact on the league. Her interest helped drive new fans to the sport. One research firm suggested that Swift's huge popularity helped earn the NFL more than $330 million during the 2023 season.

Kansas City became the eighth NFL team to win consecutive Super Bowls when it beat the 49ers in Super Bowl LVIII.

time expired. Then in the final seconds of overtime, Mahomes made his game-winning throw to Mecole Hardman for a 25–22 win.

The Chiefs returned in 2024 hoping to make NFL history. No team had ever won three straight Super Bowls. Kansas City won 15 games during the regular season, its most ever. Then they knocked off the Texans and Bills to set up a Super Bowl rematch with the Eagles. But this time, Philadelphia had the answers for Kansas City's offense. The Eagles sacked Mahomes six times. The Chiefs' star also threw two interceptions. Philadelphia ran away with a 40–22 win. The Chiefs' dream of three straight titles was over. But with so much talent on the roster, the dynasty was far from finished.

TIMELINE

1960
The Chiefs are founded by businessman Lamar Hunt as the Dallas Texans of the AFL.

1962
Dallas wins the AFL championship 20-17 in double overtime over the Houston Oilers.

1963
The Texans relocate to Kansas City and are renamed the Chiefs.

1967
After winning the AFL championship, the Chiefs lose 35-10 in Super Bowl I to the Green Bay Packers on January 15.

1970
The Chiefs upset the Minnesota Vikings 23-7 in Super Bowl IV on January 11.

1971
Kansas City loses 27-24 in double overtime to the Miami Dolphins in the longest NFL game ever played.

1990
Linebacker Derrick Thomas sets an NFL record with seven sacks in one game.

1993
The Chiefs trade for quarterback Joe Montana, who leads the team to the AFC title game.

2003
Priest Holmes sets an NFL record with 27 rushing touchdowns in one season.

2018
Second-year quarterback Patrick Mahomes becomes the first Chiefs player to win the NFL's MVP Award.

2020
The Chiefs defeat the San Francisco 49ers 31–20 on February 2, clinching Kansas City's first Super Bowl win in 50 years.

2023
Kansas City defeats the Philadelphia Eagles 38–35 to win Super Bowl LVII on February 12.

2024
On February 11, Mahomes's touchdown pass in overtime against the 49ers wins Super Bowl LVIII 25–22.

GLOSSARY

coordinator—an assistant coach who is in charge of the offense, defense, or special teams.

draft—a system that allows teams to acquire new players coming into the league.

dynamic—energetic and exciting; in sports, usually referring to an athlete with one or more outstanding skills.

dynasty—a team that has an extended period of success, usually winning multiple championships in the process.

embolism—a blockage of an artery inside a person's body.

era—a period of time in history.

franchise—an entire sports organization.

general manager—an executive who runs a team and is responsible for finding and signing players.

inaugural—marking the beginning of an institution, activity, or period of office.

merge—join with another to create something new, such as a company, a team, or a league.

motion—movement by a player from one side of an offensive formation to the other before the snap of the ball.

overtime—an extra period of play when the score is tied after regulation.

retire—to end one's career.

rookie—a professional athlete in his or her first year of competition.

sack—a tackle of the quarterback behind the line of scrimmage before he can pass the ball.

shotgun—a formation in which the quarterback lines up 5 to 7 yards behind the center and takes the snap in the air.

special teams—the players on the field for kicking and punting plays.

underdog—the person or team that is not expected to win.

versatile—able to perform many different roles or functions.

veteran—someone who has played for many years.

ONLINE RESOURCES

Booklinks
NONFICTION NETWORK
FREE! ONLINE NONFICTION RESOURCES

To learn more about the Kansas City Chiefs, please visit **abdobooklinks.com** or scan this QR code. These links are routinely monitored and updated to provide the most current information available.

INDEX